LEARNING TO SLEEP

LEARNING TO SLEEP

John Burnside

CAPE POETRY

3 5 7 9 10 8 6 4

Jonathan Cape, an imprint of Vintage, is part of the Penguin Random House group of companies whose addresses can be found at global.penguinrandomhouse.com.

Penguin
Random House
UK

First published by Jonathan Cape in 2021

penguin.co.uk/vintage

The authorised representative in the EEA is Penguin Random House Ireland, Morrison Chambers, 32 Nassau Street, Dublin D02 YH68

A CIP catalogue record for this book is available from the British Library

ISBN 9781787332348

Typeset in 11/13 pt Bembo by Jouve (UK), Milton Keynes

Printed and bound by CPI Group (UK) Ltd, Croydon, CR0 4YY

Penguin Random House is committed to a sustainable future for our business, our readers and our planet. This book is made from Forest Stewardship Council® certified paper.

for Iain Galbraith

CONTENTS

LEARNING TO SLEEP

Nous vivons encore sous le règne de la logique
André Breton

IN MEMORIAM

Tell me there is
A meadow, afterward.
Lucie Brock-Broido

Wooing is out of fashion,
like silence,
or manna,

no fervour any more, no
Tir na Nog.
The only rationale

is sainthood: love
as absence and a bloodless
hunger in the cloisters of the heart

where nothing can intrude
that is not
properly heraldic:

mercy for mercy's sake, the colour blue,
those novels where the dead wake with the dead
and go to work, thick

shadows in the frost,
a footfall in the loft that no-one hears
till someone stays her hand

and turns to listen.
If everything you love can disappear
then anything you choose could bring it back,

handfuls of dusk and grammar, plucked from the air,
a Midnight Mass
of *Tannenbaum* and silver.

Orpheus, so they say, could sing a bird
from nowhere, oriole
or turnstone, dotterel

or bar-tailed godwit rising in the mist
and flickering away
across the sands. It was

a gift he had,
a sense for halcyon
his voice could not renounce.

How many nights, I wonder,
in the untold
bliss of shaping, did he chance to sing

some unexpected life into the world?
How long before that halcyon
decayed?

I see you, now, come in out of the snow
to read the note I never got
to send
        – a waiter

slips it, surreptitiously, into
the pocket of your antique
raincoat, when you hang it up to dry

in one of the more elegant cafes
of Afterward, the rain-light
splashed across the room like early

Hopper, minimal and damp,
but touched with something not unlike
the permanence of *then* and *then again*

— a page torn from a book,
though what it says
is: *couldn't you have stayed for this*

finale, when the rain evolves
to snow, a white
kabuki in the theatre of trees

on Riverside
         — as if there was a choice
to stay, when Orpheus himself could not undo
the slither in the grass that finds us out,

each of us, one by one and, each,
alone,
having been once, *this*

once, and not again;
though (yes)
there is a Meadow
           — afterward.

EXTINCTION SUTRA/BLIND PIG BLUES

So he drove out the man; and he placed at the east of the garden of Eden cherubims, and a flaming sword which turned every way, to keep the way of the tree of life.

Genesis 3: 24

I *Nunc fluens facit tempus,*
   nunc stans facit aeternitatum

I am leaning as far as I can
into the script
of bloodline, new pups
falling in spills
from the farrow, their snouts
besmirched with a slick
of forebirth
and candied fat.
At large, and alone
in the sway
of a darkening tide,
I am learning to mourn
the saints we will never become:
snow at the back of my head
and a garment of suede
hand-stitched with lice and down
for the next
extinction.
When gods and martyrs
battle in the eaves
under a curd-white
moon, the smell of rain
is welcome, like a hymn-tune
or a letter,
and any longueur is an art

when the parting is done
and we sit up all night
with too many theories
to choose from:
the gold of the famous
past, or the *entre deux guerres*
where history comes
to a standstill, a wayward
gunshot in the beech-woods, or a wave
of plovers, rising,
green-gold in the light;
and nothing is here
that did not involve
a god, in the flawless decay
of our grandparents' garden,
a stray wisp of foxglove or daisy
rooted in clinker,
a tin-pail of potash and bone
by the breeze-block wall.
Now, stranger-in-waiting,
but kin to the sleek
autochthon who might have passed
for the last of his kind,
I am pledged to ignore the flag
for a chorus of frogs
or the stink of the dogs coming through
over pockmarked snow.
Ashamed of surviving so long
in a hireling's skin,
I occupy the dative like a fallen
mustardseed, determined to arrive
at salt and ice, all sanctuary foregone,
to go back to the Verb, and nothing else,
my brethren submerged in the earth
with the aurochs and auks,

long dynasties
of saddlebacks and lops
immersed in a rammed earth floor
with the blood of kings.

They parted the flesh and clamped it
open, vast heads
lolling away to the dark, the snapped ribs
ghosting on a silence I could hear
from sixty yards away, my windows
open to the honeysuckle lanes
of dust and musk
beneath the lightening stars.
Improbable; and yet I must have slept
an hour or more, the step-van rumbling down
the driveway, when I went to look again,
a pail of blood and matter by the door,
the sky slammed shut,
to hold that heartbeat in.

III *Quis legem det amantibus? maior lex amor est sibi*

There must be a kind of grace in mistaking
bitter for clean; say

the tang of an unripe fruit, or that undertone
of coal-tar

in the first thick draught
of snow;

how, sooner or later,
a boy winds back to the ditch

where a body has started
to darken, and yet

no history of slur
or seepage in what used to be a face

can mitigate the lapsus
of the eye.

It could be true, like fenugreek,
or gall,

though what I would have chosen to unearth
is smaller than a gift for finding

truffles:
a new life, in the tart minutiae

that someone else would relegate forthwith
to substance in its least inclusive form,

a slur of keratin, or sorrel leaf,
diminished on a windshield till it clears

on fauna too immediate
to ignore.

In one definition of the verb
'to suffer'

I find a meadow
five miles out of town,

a meadow, or a patch of no man's land,
pigmyweed clogging the pit

that was once a pool
of hornwort and flowering rushes,

Fat Hen and Pearl Everlasting
knitting the gravel,

unprepossessing, no doubt,
but better than nothing:

a hint of flex or salvage in a sprawl
of whin and bone, an unbegotten glint

of animus or kinship, something
moving, as I move, across the wind:

a creature with its own idea of sleep,
about to be extinct, *a beast so wyld,*

more lotus
than the sinkhole of the heart.

IV   A slaughterman, 1962

He must have smelled
of something, blood, or offal,
kidney dribble leaking through the film

of after-shave and soap that marked him out
as strange amongst the beasts;
standing beside the low stone

work-shed, at the near-end
of the yards, he looked
too old, a Woodbine

cradled in his lips, his head
inclined, as if to listen for a sound
that only he could hear.

On certain days, in winter, when the air
was still, I heard it too,
but didn't dare reveal

what I had guessed,
a shuffling noise, a ripple in the massed
impatience on the far side of the wall,

waiting to be despatched, for mercy's sake,
the dark heads turning, slowly, as he smoothed
his apron clean and slipped into the dark.

V Notes towards an extinction

Late in the day; and behind us the former
high road, stray dogs
hunting in the backstreets where we once
played Catch-Kiss and Blind Man's Buff
all summer long;
new Latin, like a wasps' nest on our tongues,
plant names and pax vobiscum, Roman gods,
Albertus Magnus singing down the years.

Calculus shadowed our mornings, tender as sin;
but, mostly, we were schooled
in absence, at our best
in languages we never hoped to learn: Brythonic
burring on the tongue, from church to home,
mere lamplight in the house and nothing
animate, no starlings in the roof,
no field mice in the cupboard understairs;

so, now, there is no end
to what we know,
though what we know
is never quite enough
to set things right:
the catechismal rot between the leaves
of *Moonfleet*, or *The London Almanac*,
the short shrift of a casual fathering;

and still no easy way
to say goodbye:
story as last resort, repentance as fabric;
that linger, like a footfall in the Rock

of Ages, when we lift our eyes to see
the megafauna, bright as cherubim,
gone down into the flood
and still not drowned.

FOUR VARIATIONS ON
THE MANCHURIAN CANDIDATE

But my dear fellow, we don't need interpreters here.
We all speak the same language.
'Raymond Shaw', in *The Manchurian Candidate*

I

Lately, there's been a glitch in the present tense,
the blackbird calling from the holly tree
and that frost-scent on the wind in late July,
a spindrift from the east that finds me out
as stranger to the soul
I took for granted;

II

and lately, I am troubled in the night,
aroused from a dream of God, like a monk from his cell,
to map a flight of bees from glebe
to glebe, the oak-woods
harbouring those guests our fathers knew
by name, the meadows
quickening with clouds of Speckled Wood,
Dingy Skipper, Large White, Holly Blue.

III

This is the season for fetching the past from its lair
and setting it out on a table to be admired,
a great *ikebana* of lilies and pink carnations,
beauty by misadventure, ritual love:

IV

a glitch in the script where the childhood I barely remember
is mansion enough to house a communion of saints:
the erstwhile, the shop-soiled, the steadfast, the self-deceived,
the beauteous martyrs I kept in the attic like lodgers,
clerics in topcoats and scarves in the heat of the night
and the sisters I gladly betrayed for a role in the movie
come home from the woods after years
for the final cut.

FAKE COCHINEAL

We played that game of dying like the fade
of rainfall in a small apartment block
in Cracow
                    – which I think we must have known
from motion pictures –

                              not the kind of place
to grow wisteria, though something in the sound
the pigeons made would have us think again
of last year's gold.

And so it darkened: trampled leaves and snow
like scabs of moonlight wasting in a crown
of butcher's broom.

It only took one wolf to make the forest
large again, a splash of sandalwood
to parse a finch, a suitcase on the stairs,

then, later, in the cutting, wakeful dogs
and empty boxcars, bright with frost and lye.

ASPECTS OF MENTAL ECONOMY

At last the Mothering has come indoors,
tracking the walls with glitz from an old
Compendium of Fairy Tale and Fable;

summer in every stairwell, bottles
perched on windowsills, a blackbird
calling from the furthest edge of dawn.

If nobody expected it to be
so final, like the red beneath a nail
in any crucifixion where the god

is bartered for a memory of now,
at least we have the maps we learned to draw
through years of goad

and witness, no
formality so perfect as this ink
that cancels out the territory for miles:

the church we know from sleep, the market cross,
the fare-thee-well implicit in a dance
where anyone might blunder into Thou.

AN ANGEL PASSES

No one is here for once upon a time,
so if the hour is now, put up your book
and listen, while the angel does its spiel,
if not, stay as you were, the light
re-spinstering your face
by slow degrees, your fingers
tangled in a myth of needlecraft,
love without liking, Prussian without the blue,
the boys of summer, featureless and white,
calling, in *Sermo Vulgaris,* these thoughts and prayers
from long ago, when someone held you dear.

ODE TO HYPNOS

Here is the angel of slumber, come from the woods
to press a bloody talon to the glass;
the erstwhile abolitionist
of *mardi gras*, pure stranger to himself,
he fabricates this ersatz
Eden, trading bishoprics of light
for milk and honey, words in Aramaic,
a *Weihnachtsmarkt*
of diet pills and Lauds.

Here is the house of the echo, and here
the boys clothed all-in-green, the moonshine
flaking from their bones
forevermore,
a troupe of all the souls
we might have been,
crossing the seven bridges, one by one,
like Struwwelpeter dolls, with ink for skin
and nothing to keep them from hurt
but the promise of dawn.

HETHER BLETHER

for Erland Cooper

No way of knowing for sure
that the story is true:
a lost girl walking away
in the first grey light,
daughter, or sister,
crossing an open field
with a basket of apples:
there for a moment, then

vanished, a gap
too sudden to be
altogether final;
and yet, the days
run on, her laughter
fading, silence
hanging in the hallway
like a fog.

And where is the father
or brother who never dismissed
the likeness of
some half-life in himself,
some rumour of a silkie carried home
from childhood, bright
and fleeting as the first rose
of the year?

In the kingdom of myth,
her body remembers itself

as somebody's ghost:
wet sleet falling for days
at a faraway window;
no mothering
brimful enough
to guide her, when she

dips into the blue
of utterance, still
cradling a sip
of honey
from the hive
she left untold,
a memory
traced all the way

to childhood
and the last bright
summer, grasses
golden to the root, a kestrel
hunting in a wind she always
thought of
as particular
to home.

Years may go by; they
hear her through the tides,
not quite the call they
wanted, thin
and distant
like that ache
behind the lungs
that never comes to song;

but out on the sea lanes, farther
than compass or chart,
a bell rings close at hand,
or so it seems;
or else: a voice
from nowhere, bright
and sudden
in a sudden bank of haar,

and still the men go
fishing in their low, wide
vessels, at the far edge
of their world,
searching for some new
harbour, where the seal-folk
gather close to shore, their faces
silent, and sad,

as we are, and yet
so graceful,
when they venture
from the herd,
so graceful and so
like, as we are like,
that any man
could think of them
as kin.

SILKIE

At midnight, when I rise, insomniac,
and go down to the kitchen for a glass
of water (bars of moonlight in the blinds; the wall-clock
halted, months ago, at seven ten)

I know that, by the force of some
new geography that I have yet to learn,
a woman will be standing at the sink,
gutting a basket of cod, the fish-scales

slick on her hands, the hollows of her eyes
a blue that I have never seen before.
And this is where the cruelty begins,
in cleverness and lust and frayed desire,

not for this creature, who turns from the ache of the tide,
then fritters away the moment I touch her hand,
but someone to come, in the lists of the unforeseen,
who forfeits her skin for a lifetime of moonshine and gospel.

LEARNING TO SLEEP

Though the hunter returns
at first light, bearing a heart

in which all warmth
has ceased, the gut hook

sticky in his hand, his misdeed
visible to everyone he meets

– the horseman on the road,
the miller's girl,

the foreign delegation with its gold
and ermines, sundry

pilgrims, crowding
the taverns, their garments

bloody and pockmarked
with wax – the fact remains

that no one but the Queen
can ever know

the half of it:
how something in the glass

has stopped forever, setting love aside
so coldly, she could reinvent herself

as Rose-Red, while the hunter
turns away,

leaving the heart, like a bud
that has still to break,

and rinsing the glit from his knife
in a fluster of ice.

STUDIO WEATHER

for Gil

– by which my younger son means
days like this:
driving across the ridge, the far sky
black as ink, the foreground
lit, as if from nowhere,
thunder beyond a field of oilseed rape, bright
sunlight facing.

I've only just begun
to notice how he makes up names
for everything he fears I might have missed;
busy with being old, busy with care,
I don't see how the daffodils become
more yellow in the run-up to the storm
until he points it out,

or, when the rain comes, dark and inexplicably
triumphant, in the woods
around Lathockar,
it finds an unexpected hoard
of gravity, an old avoirdupois
deep in the bones of our hands, and he looks at me
as if he thinks I'll never feel again,

the world running on without me, studio weather,
bright rain spotting the dust in a stand
of nettles, as we turn into the yard
and something else flickers away
from the swing of our headlamps,
a body we cannot describe
till we know it is gone.

ON BEING PAGAN

I   On the animal familiar

We have yet to consider the heart
as animal, the totem we forgot

in Bible Class, when everything we knew
was broadcast back to us

as purple noise.
Small rain pitted the windows, years of dreaming

settled on the glass
like spots of dust,

and still, uncanticled, it filled the room:
wolf in the shadows, mongoose in the light,

a barn owl floating softly through the psalms,
until it found its prey, a single word

plucked lifelike from the air
in one fell swoop

and shredded, on the cusp
of alleluia.

II   Incarnation

It had nothing to do with the beauty
of neon, or the strings of Chinese

lanterns, dragon-blue
and plum-red in the trees around the square;

and though we stayed up late
for years, we never

thought of it as time, preoccupied
with loopholes in the story, streaks

of alomancy bleeding through the wind,
and how the Masters

brought the Sacred Heart
to light, the more

incarnadine, the more
it silvered in its sheath of summer rain;

and nothing so cruel
as when the sunlight

warmed us, on that patch of moss and grit
behind St John's,

the bud-break
in our veins a vague undoing,

snow at the fence line, Hallowmas
ghosting the walls,

the owl on the low road,
lost in the shortfall of Now.

III   The Old Masters

About suffering, they knew no more or less
than we do, being

housed in luminescence;
a local cumulus

of feverfew and jade
reduced to void, *the tower overthrown,*

the bells upturned.
I see one now, impoverished

and old before his time, a lesser man's
subordinate, or master to a trade

he never asked for.
Burdened by the weight

of office, or the whim of some mad king,
he stands alone, above a dark lagoon,

and watches, while the city fades from quartz
to plum, from plum

to cochineal, a restless drift
through subtleties and shades

he cannot
capture, though he magnifies the whole

and loves it all the more for being
useless, fleeting, governed by no rule,

a headlong and unmasterable now
that slips away, one pier light at a time.

IV   Si peu de choses

We are close to the final end
of *ding an sich*,
a shortfall in those presences
that once seemed
urgent, merest
namesakes
in a field of Cobalt Blue.
Nostalgia for Beauteous
Being, splinter cells
of Crimson Lake
and Flake White
gone to dust,
abandoned car-wrecks in a pool
of nettles, fishnets
snagged with requiem
and faded bone.
The Star of Bethlehem.
The Southern Cross.
What passes, in this realm,
for solid matter.
Some pathos in the way
the torn heart clings to ruin,
but nothing we can count on, save the sweet
dilemma of a blackbird in the hall, the lovely
panic in that longing for the sky;
yet let it be taken as read that life goes on,
a series of interruptions, but nothing cancelled,
even if, now and then,
at intervals less random than they seem,
an instance surrenders its place
to something other.
Out in the dark,

a ribbon of light and perish,
but nothing gained or lost, no harvest moon
or Sabbath yet to come,
and I think, at the end,
we remember no more than a garden:
hortensias spotted with rain, a passing thrush,
crab apples, roses, lullabies ghosting the walls,
the city around us, tragic and burlesque,
going about its business, ad infinitum.

TOXIC

VLADIMIR:
Suppose we repented.

ESTRAGON
Repented what?

VLADIMIR:
Oh ... (He reflects.) We wouldn't have to go into the details.

Samuel Beckett, *Waiting for Godot*

AFFIANCED BY OATH

Rain at the gates and here she is again:
ragazza of the northlands, part-
acetylene, part-

mother, she will teach him how to love
not wisely,
but too well;

and why he can't be kind is just a map
he never learned to read, though he could tell
one landmark from another, killing floor

from chapel in the woods, the low road
vanishing at times into the mire
that waits to be resumed, the way the heart

resumes its darkest form and hunkers down,
to feed on any sweetmeat it can find.

THE MODERN DANCE

Heart like a fledgling wren, and yet
less Thou than he had looked for, she is
spouse elect, but never quite The Bride.

Now he goes back to sleeping, like
the princess he pretended to disdain
when others told the story and he dreamed

how happy-ever-after it might be
had he but found the wherewithal to lie
with something other than an empty gown.

THE PRICE OF SAND

We are bits of stellar matter that got cold by accident,
bits of a star gone wrong.

Arthur Stanley Eddington

To speak of the borrowed mother, if I may,
her small perfections all about the house, that

dumb-show in the hallway where the light
is neatened with a vase of antirrhinums.

How can she be so purely surrogate?
the warmth of a cradled palm, or a sun-bruised

collar, strictly code-red on this Mount
of Olives that, on maps, they always show

as no man's land;
and no man's land is hers, beyond a doubt,

though sleep is something else, pledged to sateen
and similes comparing all she is

to dusk and fur:
the corpus of a girlhood in the woods;

the moth she sometimes barters for a heart.

TOXIQUE

In solitary, though always *so to speak*,
Empress of starvelings, couched in the Chinese White
of moonrise, till the first light turns to frost
and everything she ever learned to add
for sweetness, every sugar-spiced and snag-toothed
poppet she could conjure from the night
spills from her gown like a bushel of summer grain.
Virgin again, she trails home after dark,
with salt-stains on her dress and some new word
for Paraclete, like venom on her tongue,
and whoso list to hunt shall dim his blade
for pity's sake, that she might play the Queen.

TOXIC

I saw him in the mist
by Sutton's Pool,

a boy I could barely
imagine: kit bag

swollen with guddled
trout, he flicked

a match into the grass
and walked away.

No footprints in the dew,
no mark at all,

only a wisp of smoke
in the evening fog

and a faraway
whistle.

Midsummer's Eve, he
leans in for a kiss,

my step-sister
squirming away, his eyes

on me:
the smell of diesel

filming on his skin,
his small disdain

a gift
from the hereafter.

A BRIEF MEMO, FOR VALENTINE'S DAY

There was something lodged in my chest.
It felt like bone.
I peeled back the skin and levered –
gently, at first – then I drew it
all the way out, with my grandmother's
snub-nosed pliers. Ivory-white

and smoother than the wounds that we would kiss
on Holy Days,
it seemed that, once, this object might have been,
if not alive, then part of something whole,
some shared mind, like a colony of bees
or Giant Northern Termites;

and, just for a moment, I thought it might
come to life,
the way, in a folk tale, the Raven will speak its name
or all the world will sing in unison.
But nothing happened, other than a faint
and barely legible discoloration.

I buried it out in the paddock,
under a thorn,
then stood a long time gazing at the moon.
As if I could have measured what was lost;
or told how sweet it is
to be alive.

A CHANGELING

How ravished one could be without ever being touched.
Ravished by dead words become obscene and dead ideas
become obsessions.

D. H. Lawrence

In the fields between Foulford Burn
and the Crook of Devon,
the boy I had been went astray, and was never found
by the men of that place, who promised to fetch him home
intact and unharmed, before the first blue of evening.

No one would ever have said
that my absence was close
to exquisite, the void shirt
dripping on the line, the bed turned down,
the curve of the box-room, under the devious stars;

and nobody pretended to believe
when word came of my perfect
likeness in the back seat of an Austin
Cambridge, all the toffees I'd refused
preserved in a tamper-proof bag for the deposition.

If only I'd known, I could have walked away,
but home is where they have to take you in
and I was perfect altar boy
material, my body cold as stone, and in my eyes,
a look that said I'd do it all again;

and though they said I wasn't there for good,
I stayed away for reasons of my own,
a shadow in the wildwood, laying snares
for creatures long-extinct, with just a trace
of caramel and Woodbine on my hands.

A LONG ENGAGEMENT

When I think of the *Mädchen* she hides
in neck-scarves and fingerless gloves,

her finite beauty
delicate, and presently

endangered, like a live mouse
in a snare,

I want to leave this church and be reborn
as one of those old friars in his cell

who grinds up stones
for colour, soft,

mercuric undertones
to light the trails of violet and rue

unroping through his bishop's
Book of Hours.

How long ago our names were written there,
between a turning swallow and a type

of bat no longer found much in these parts,
I couldn't say.

It seems a lifetime
since that game began:

a flock of echoes dipping through a maze
of Timothy and foxtails, while the farm-cats

plucked them from the memory of air,
so tenderly, you'd think their god had wings.

A LADY OF THE PARISH

Purest *comadre*, sun-slicked in her weeds,
she snares you in The Book of *Très Riches Heures*
at Whitsun, part-exemption, part-reprieve,
a speck of gold-leaf flaking on her skin
to chalk and foil.
                No saints' days
in the backrooms of her heart,
only the priest's house, busy with must and tallow,
a Rambling Rector wreathed around the porch,
fishnets and creels in the yard, like something
memorised from Oberammergau,
where everything is lost, to start again:
the foundling in the vestry, wrapped in silks,
a Boy King, in his interlude of tar.

TO THE YOUNGER MAN

I see you know
    the world's way, all that

slop and carrion
    of having, but not

being.
    Ludic and cavalier, you're almost

viable
    in someone else's hell,

answering dog
    with shark, aristocrat

with *nunc dimittis;*
    but rest assured,

you're welcome in this place,
    there's no one, here, would

Ides of March
    your party;

and, listen:
    you can hear it in the floor,

that clatter
    when you stumble out of luck,

a tiny brightness,
    like a fallen coin.

So no one's asking you
    to tell the truth,

just don't pretend
  you walked into a fate

you knew
  would happen;

there's falcon still to come,
  the noontide

swing of it, before the claws
  dig in;

and later, when it dives
  to drain the heart

and daybreak finds you
  with a run of blood,

like grease, between your collar
  and your chin,

step out into the sun
  for all to see:

your friends,
  your dead, this

team
  of publicans,

the ones you loved
  and those you never knew

who only kept you sweet,
  to gut you now.

WHOSO LIST TO HUNT

Small comfort to be had in *mea culpa*,
damp afternoons, just shy
of saccharine,
re-scripted as a cyclopaedia
of catechismal storms
and venial sins.
No subtlety of eyes around my bed;
no whispered blame, no frost-fall in the blood,
but later, when I lay me down to sleep
and all the lamps burn out across the yards,
I waken to the sadness of the creatures:
love in the absence of Thou, the finer
disciplines that winter recommends.
Such refuge as I find, but cannot keep,
since in a net I seek to hold the wind.

NEVER THE BRIDE

She dies into the green we've come to know
from psaltery and years of Outside

Broadcast, thumbprints
broidered to the beauty

of her skin, a safe word
printed on each wrist,

but not disclosed.
No princess in this dress, and no

Madonna; neither
Sphinx nor Echo, she alone persists:

a pink that comes to mind
when all else fails,

a trace of sandalwood or *fleur-de-lys*
meandering

through candy-stripe
and sinew.

A hair's breadth from the knife,
she makes her peace

with nightfall,
while the perfume on her lips

entices the huntsman back
to the dowager's palace.

Or, far from home,
in minarets of ice,

she lies down in her bed
of small disdain,

her gown in shreds,
her happiness complete,

a flame in her heart
for the forfeit she paid to the hounds.

THE DAYS

Les jours s'en vont je demeure
Guillaume Apollinaire

INDELIBLE

I should like De Haan to see a study of mine of a lighted candle and two novels (one yellow, the other pink) lying on an empty chair (really Gauguin's chair), a size 30 canvas, in red and green. I have just been working again today on its pendant, my own empty chair, a white deal chair with a pipe and a tobacco pouch. In these two studies, as in others, I have tried for an effect of light by means of clear colour, probably De Haan would understand exactly what I was trying to get if you read to him what I have written on the subject.

Vincent van Gogh, Letter to Theo, 17 January 1889

I   English Speaking Board, 1968

There was something I heard in an early
ballad:
     a life
less sense
than sound;

the ghost of a word, like a bird's egg
cracking against my tongue, the sweetness
brimful in my throat;

         but that
was long ago, before I learned by chance
to hold things dear.

Sometimes I heard it clear
in the snowbound gap
between HOME and LIGHT,

the radio warm and live
in my mother's kitchen,

a place name, a shift in the weather,
our dialect of love
and common prayer,

hand-me-down terms for the heave
of a pit-shaft wall

or the sputter and flare of the wick
in a starboard lantern.

At times, it had something to do
with the click and roll
of snooker, in those smoke and sea-green rooms

above the library, the scent of working men
distilled to malt and Capstan Navy Cut;

sometimes it came through the air
on a summer's dawn,
when we counted the boats going out
from a starlit harbour,

and though it was barely
an echo, a song without words,
the meaning was always clear, its pledge

precise as the wandering bees
in some Sweet
Hereafter.

We filmed those days
in memory and light:

the sea in its garment
of signals: semaphore; wireless;

fog warnings sifted through miles
of moonshine and ether,

that fall in the wind
like the stalled heart coming to grief

no more than a moment's
lull, or the hyperacoustic
simmer in the hollow of a bell;

backroads through wheel-churn and snow
a mile from Lumphinnans,

a harvest of mint
and plums, on the path to Loch Fitty
                              – the place names
tangle and burr on my tongue, these decades later,

the language no longer mine, the illusive
gravity of RP at my back,
though not in the least

convincing: *The rain in Spain* . . .
My father's car (why not?) *is a Jaguar* . . .

For English Speaking Board, they taught me
not just to speak, but to think in a mother tongue
my mother never knew, a genteel

proxy for our pagan dialect
of locked grimoires
and backstreet skipping rhymes,

collective nouns
for shore birds, new snow

blown through the scullery door, when my mother
sent me to fetch the coal
on a Christmas morning.

I have the certificate still

                                    and the lingering sense
that I once had a word
for how the snowmelt

freezes, then melts, then
freezes again on a clutch
of rosehips or native thorn,

or how in the middle of winter,
the colour deepens,
no longer bright, like
the blood of their slaughtered god,

but stubborn as an ember in the wind
– earthbound, human, rare as any spark –
that never catches fire
but will not perish.

II   Matinee, 1963

After the show, we drive home in the dark,
like children sleeping in another world
who dream of a relentless *vérité*
that never lets its guard down; every
named thing in its place
ein feste Burg: the chapel in the woods,
velour and rain as stand-ins for the heart.

Why one thing seems important, when it's all
the same is just the mystery we learn
from having nothing, always making good:
a street lamp on the corner where the trees
close in, though just a little, so the light
seems blessed by something other than the god
we had to know for school; or that one stretch

of back road, running out across the fields
through perfect blackness, till it found the turn
where Minto Pit stood tethered to the stars,
like some great barge of fire and beaten gold.

III   Indelible

Summer again. A girl skips rope in the street
while her friend keeps time.
The neighbour's azaleas
put out their hairstreaked blossoms,
a plausible fragrance, summoning the bees
from every park and yard
for miles around,
and my mother is slicing a heart
at the kitchen table:
sixty years past, and today, the side door
open to the part-songs of the birds,
lilac in drifts and shoals along the alley,
the old year black in the gutter, the new rain pooled
on miles of light from here to Cowdenbeath,
shop-fronts and Miners' Rescue, my several uncles
catching the bus to Lauder for Technical Drawing,
lights on the tram to Dunfermline, lamps at the pit-heads,
ships' lanterns far on the water, the Rail Bridge
lit all the way to Hopetoun and Davidson's Mains
– and my mother is slicing a heart
in my empty kitchen:
the radio tuned to HOME, a handful of flour
sprinkled across the table, the music low,
she works as she always did, absorbed in her task,
her chef's-knife catching the light
as she trims the gristle.

I've never believed in ghosts, and I've no great wish
to harbour the dead
– and besides, if she spoke, I'm not sure I'd understand,
a language between us now, a willed forgetting;
but how could I not respect what refuses to fade,

like the blur in the paint where a hand or a porcelain bowl
conceals the *pentimento* of a tethered
songbird?
How could the boy in my shoes quite disbelieve
what they told him about
the friend of a friend of a friend
who witnessed a light that nobody could explain,
a lucency over the pond where, year after year,
the baker's son fell through the ice,
when no-one was watching?

For a moment the music stops and my mother
angles her head to listen, one more song
from sixty years ago:
a falling star, a many-splendored thing
– and I see her again, caught up in a sudden fog,
the summer her youngest died, a saint's name
taken in vain, the light of him rumoured, then gone.
We are out for a Sunday walk, on the path by the burn,
and she in the green print dress that she loved to wear,
green as the riverweed, drawn through the green of the current
– and now that I think, it's the colour that pulls me back,
the *verde que te quiero* that never
ceases, while the current pushes on
till, just for a moment, I reach out to stay the blade,
her hand almost there in my hand as I try to explain
that we never eat heart any more, or not
in this house;
we never eat liver, or tripe,
or pigs' trotters simmered for hours
to draw out the flavour.

But when I look again to where she was,
my mother is gone and the chair
is empty, like the dead space in a wood
after a tree is felled, or to be more precise,

like the chair in the famous van Gogh, the 'empty place' he painted when Gauguin left, the light from the gas lamp blue on the polished wood and the stem of the candle, perfectly clear and almost too pale to endure.

RATIONING FOR BEGINNERS

When it no longer smells like an orchard
gathering around me in the dark,
the sense of a known Beloved that comes
of garden work, the honey of a voice
receding in my throat, my flesh
more sleep than dream;

when nothing on the air
gives answer to that hollow in the bone
from years ago, the wound I never told,
no scar to show
by daylight, nothing
Ancient in my house, or Perilous;

when flocks of geese rise,
month-long, from the fields
and arc towards the north,
I'll say I drowned my books, then start again,
for no-one's sake,
one heartbeat at a time.

My mother is a day's walk in the rain,
waiting for someone to come
with pear-drops and nylons;
my father is a gun beyond the hill,
his shirtsleeves hemmed and seamed
with sweet molasses,

but neither knows the childhood I will spin
from laughing gas
and mild diphtheria,
the dreams I'll furnish
on the bus ride home
more gospel than I know, a house of lights

where all our yesterdays lie side by side
in narrow beds, from Loos to Belleau Wood,
and when the rain goes by, the April sun
blooms on their hands and mine, a passing gleam,
just permanent enough to warm my skin
in lieu of presence, text-book, like the gods.

AT NOTRE DAME DE REIMS

the snake
is a snake;

but the toad has a human face, in the hidden
gallery under the roof, where the masons

practised their art, away from the bishops
and kings.

We've seen this much before (in Salisbury, say,
or that chapel above the Esk

at Rosslyn):
a refuge for the pagan in the chill

of Christendom, a Green Man
in the fabric of the stone; a running

boar; the sacred
hare; or else

the common wren, so
lifelike it might flit at any time

to nest in the deepest corner, tail
erect, the eye

agleam, as if to indicate
its known propensity

for lust
(which, in the old tongue, meant no more

than pleasure: no-one's
shame and not a sin,

but life as such, immediate
and true

like flight,
or song).

At Reims,
they say,

the toad is done
from life – *sans doute*

un proche – a relative
or friend,

and high in the highest beams,
where no one goes,

a workman has sculpted a cat
with a woman's smile.

It's cold in here: a memory of life,
not life itself,

just as the light
that falls through the stained-glass

window falls
to scattered points of colour in the dark,

not from a god, but from a common
memory of being

lost amongst the trees, old demons
watching from the murk,

an errant body
flitting back and forth

till something more familiar
than a god

escorts the wanderer home
- no shame in that,

nor any sin: a rabbit for the pot,
a brace of quail,

and nothing to confess,
should there be warmth

and laughter in the house
(a hut, no more,

under the cold facade
their hands have raised

to someone else's god, a stone
conclusion,

while the old life
bides its time)

nothing to be refused,
where there is hearth

and humour
and the fleet

mysterium that runs
from skin to skin:

a mischief in the eye,
a sly remark,

a live cat
lapping the cream

while the stew-pot
simmers.

I PROMESSI SPOSI IN THE HOME
COUNTIES, AUGUST 1993

A sub-plot brought them here, to count the days
in suburbs built of fibreglass

and timber;
a garden of their own, a serpentine

of hosepipe in the grass, the minor
Kyries of saints' days, traded up

for midnight in the glad protectorate
of only here in passing.

They say the heart grows frugal at the end,
like any scavenger;

pledged to the local
weather, more

conversant with the dead
than with the living;

and wedlock falls out of fashion,
like bliss, or sin,

no bridal veil, no silk *jarretière;*
no dolly of your own, stitched to the clouds,

her fingers burned
with sugarcraft and fuchsia.

ARTHUR RIMBAUD AT
SCAMBLESBY*, 1873

There is no evidence that Rimbaud ever visited Scarborough.
Graham Robb

At times, it feels like someone else's dream,
copious rain, when it comes, and the sense
of Godhead in every tongue of flame
and hymnsong in the sky above the fen;

and nightfall, in the gaps between the hills,
as quick and unrelenting as the mouth
that glides out from the ditch, no voice to tell
what symmetry it brings.

A new guest, he understands nothing:
the language; the parcelled food; the hands of the women;
the girl who serves breakfast, that coldwater light in her eyes
a death-threat, or an effort at flirtation.

Sheep watch him pass like churchgoers watching the priest
as he mutters the *corpus meum* into his sleeve,
not quite convinced, but just for a moment, stirred
by a sense of occasion.

At noon, he walks away to where the gods
who used to rule this land still haunt the roads:
Wotan in beggar's rags, a jug of cider
sunk in the ample pocket of his coat,

* A small town in Lincolnshire. There is no evidence that Rimbaud ever visited
Scamblesby.

a drunk, like any other, but for the fret
of light in his one good eye
and the longing he can't quite conceal
for some kind of mother;

or Freyja, walking home
at evening, in her kestrel-feather gown,
a basket on her arm, of leeks and plums,
a summer-long

delirium, implicit in the bloom
of damsons, or that blatant stain
of mulberry,
like goose blood on her chin.

One night he finds he is lost
on a moonlit lane
that seems to run forever through a land
that looks like the land

he came from, empty and grey
and one spire much like another;
and all he can do is follow, the path leading down
and away, through a huddle of thorns,

to a windless sky,
far from the church gate,
forgotten in folk song and fable,
where nothing seems once and for all but the proximate gold

of the final extinction:
a slow burn of leather and bone, like the slaughterhouse fire,
that once, on the road to perdition,
he traded for home.

MA BOHÈME (AFTER RIMBAUD)

Je m'en allais, les poings dans mes poches crevées;
Mon paletot aussi devenait idéal

Arthur Rimbaud

I will leave in my ideal coat,
bright as the day I learned to take light for a sign
of nothing but itself:
                no hinterland
of apropos
or corn dolls etched in steel,
no scar on the corpus callosum from fifty years
of Calculus
and Deuteronomy.

Summer again;
               the meadow is drawing in
and no one can deny the animals,
each in its pocket of rainfall
and *quatre épices*, a streak
of tenderness for everything that wanders;
and, always, the sense
that something has still to appear,
some widow-maker, come in from the fields,
with nothing on its tongue
but lullaby.

Night in the cities; lockdown; the end of neon;
simples of pus and feverfew ranged on the shelves
with spent bulbs and dog-eared
copies of *Dao De Jing*,
yarrow stalks, tea-dregs, Tarot cards spotted with wax,
Justice Reversed, Fortuna,
The Queen of Wands

– what it means, I suppose,
is that presence no longer abides,
or not in the shapes we sacrificed so much
to barter with, a twilight flooding in
from nowhere to the child-sized Shangri-La
of tree-line, where we magnify the rain
in lieu of Seraphim,
and all the smaller fauna of the age
come out into the open, where we cannot
name them; we,
who never quite achieved
the brusque humility
to be involved.

No catechism here;
no sunken church;
and yet, it seems
this mystery is ours
as ruins are, a counterpoint to grace
where each thing hunts
its echo, fish,
then fowl, first
one, and then
another: little owl
and vixen, herons
stock-still in the reeds, the stoat
unclasping from its lookout in the wall,
a thinning streak
of mastery
and venom.

The Silk Road is gone from our hearts, a final
spindrift under the concourse
of Yorkstone
and camber;

the Dreamtime is lost
                        and The Temple of Baal-Shamin;
the forests are gone to palm-oil
and Merbau decking

and all that remains of presence
is pure decorum:
no Hop-o'-My-Thumb,
no child's-play,
no Dog Shark Mother;
the Inn at the Plough
is closed, now, for renovation,

first signs of snow
on the high road, the last of the traffic
making for home, wet
blister-packs of search-lamp in the dark,
flatbeds and semis
loaded with gravel and lumber,
a last bus, bound for the depot at who knows where
– and I go my way, learning to breathe, like a Seventh Son,
wind in my head
and the murmur of stars in my blood,
till the night dew falls through the trees
like ice on my skin,
sweeter than ruin, and cool,
like a fine young wine.

PREPARATIONS FOR THE TRUE
APOCALYPSE

It is the true Apocalypse this, when the 'Open Secret' becomes revealed to a man. I rejoice much in the glad serenity of soul with which you look out on this wondrous Dwelling-place of yours and mine – with an ear for the 'Ewigen Melodien' which pipe in the winds round us, and utter themselves forth in all sounds and sights and things: not to be written down by gamut-machinery; but which all right writing is a kind of attempt to write down.
Thomas Carlyle, letter to Ralph Waldo Emerson, 13 February 1837

We have come to the last *bohème*
of being here, and still no guarantee
of other bodies, pressing through the fog

to meet us.
          Harvest, at last.
Or else, an early frost;
no alchemy so tender as the nub

of ruin, where the first plums start to fall
in long-abandoned orchards, stray
anemones and houseleeks in the weeds,

a minaret
of wasps
between the trees.

Imagine how it looks
when we are gone,
the other presences so well-achieved

they want for nothing, goldcrest in the pines,
the larger fauna, ponies
out to grass;

73

and everything that might have been undone
resuming, in the gaps we leave behind:
wave after wave of brightness on the land:

buckthorn and nightshade engulfing the last cracked wall,
black as the earth
in which our dreams are laid.

CAIRN

– as the warm egg cradles its yolk,
so Maeshowe cradles the gold
of a winter sun;
and we, who believe
in nothing but superstition,
bring out the dead in our hearts
to be born again.

AT LOCHTY BRIDGE, EAST FIFE, JANUARY 2019

Qui vivit in aeternum creavit omnia simul.

Turn of the year,
        but the snow we've been promised for weeks
has yet to arrive, the near sky

        grey as the lead
on a church roof, and no
        horizon to speak of;

pink-footed geese
        on the top ridge, wagtails
scouting the ruts

        and puddles, gulls
and oystercatchers,
        come up from the shore,

but nothing to see
        at Knightsward, the windows
empty, the yards

        abandoned for weeks and a single
buzzard tracking the path
        to the hump-backed bridge.

Once they would ship whole
        families in
from the pit towns,

women and children
working all day
for pennies, their knuckles

ice-cold and scabbed
with loam;
now it is quiet

and still:
no wind from the east,
no songbirds or passing cars

and nothing to see
but a maunder of ghost-eyed
Cheviots, cropping the verge

through a corner post, bodies
contorted, their orthodox faces
strictured and mildly indignant

like latter-day saints
– and maybe they are saintlike,
in their way,

as I might be,
if I could shed my doubts,
here, in a place

where anything can seem
a blessing:
deer coming through

from Lathockar, their faces
tender and curious, scenting me
out of the gloom,

the high stars, or an unexpected run
        of hard sleet, drifting blindly till it finds
this porch-lamp, breaking

        blue beneath the blue, a heretofore
I half-recall
        from when the world was told

as gravity and light, the gospel
        brimming from a *tairsgear,*
charged with life,

        like the liquor that pools on the floor
of a stink-pit, slow sift
        gathering like code beneath a squall

of pelt and bone, a cursive black as ink
        and legible, from one verse to the next,
as scripture, or the sweet wrath of a god.

READING DAVID HUME AT THE SUMMER SOLSTICE, EAST FIFE, 2019

Market has been and gone, the calves
dispatched, cows
bawling from yard to yard
in the summer fog.

Ghost season; just for a while, the whiteness
thinning to reveal
some *cul de sac*
that pulls our bodies in

until it feels like
presence: ours, not ours,
it's neither here nor there, once we concede
that everything we know is what it seems.

POSTSCRIPT

An evening like any other, storm clouds
stalled above the fields, my neighbour's cattle
gathered at the near edge of their known
dominion, one last tractor
dawdling to the yard, its headlights
blurring in a burst of summer rain;
and something's coming, something
sensed, but not yet seen, before the night
engulfs us and the cattle turn away,
bemused, or unconvinced, or simply
waiting for this weather to be done,
and I am with them, here, but on the brink
of elsewhere, gazing out across the land,
as if a better world was still to come.

NOTES & ACKNOWLEDGEMENTS

In Memoriam

This poem, to the memory of Lucie Brock-Broido (who died on 6 March 2018) draws on lines from her poem, 'Did Not Come Back', published in her 1995 collection, *The Master Letters.*

Extinction Sutra / Blind Pig Blues

Titles from the first and third sections of this sequence derive from Boethius' *De consolatione philosophiae*, which was written in prison during the year 523, while its author was awaiting execution.

The second section takes as its title a line from 'Blind Pig Blues', by twelve-string guitarist and Piedmont blues singer, Robert Hicks, aka Barbecue Bob, who died of influenza, aged 29, in 1932. Also attributed to Spencer Williams, the song was recorded by Hicks in Atlanta, Georgia, on 13 April 1928.

The Boethius lines are well-known, though both present difficulties when translated into English.

Quis legem det amantibus? maior lex amor est sibi; for best results, apply Chaucer's translation: 'But what is he that may yive a lawe to loveres? Love is a gretter lawe and a strenger to himself than any lawe that men may yeven.'

Nunc fluens facit tempus, nunc stans facit aeternitatum can be rendered (roughly) as: 'The Now that flows generates Time, the Now that stands generates Eternity.'

Barbecue Bob's ideas on time are perhaps best expressed in the 1930 cut, 'The Spider and the Fly Blues':

Up said the spider: to the little fly one day
Won't you come around: let's pass the time away
[. . .]
Come into my parlor: said the spider to the fly
I'll give you loving: loving until you die

Hether Blether

I am indebted to Erland Cooper for this 'lost girl' story, which
originates on the island of Rousay. For similar accounts, see Ernest
Marwick's *The Folklore of Orkney and Shetland* (1975).

Happiness as Default Setting

See T. S. Eliot, 'The Dry Salvages': 'The hint half guessed, the gift
half understood, is Incarnation.' 'The Old Masters' incorporates
lines from Eliot's 'The Rock' Choruses.

Indelible

From *The Times of Malta*, 7 June 2009: 'The English Speaking
Board was set up in England in 1953 with the aim of giving young
people the chance to develop two important life skills – speaking
and listening – which help improve self-confidence. [. . .] There are
four sections in an ESB assessment. Firstly, students are asked to
give an oral presentation based on their personal experience, voca-
tional or other interests, appropriately illustrated with visual aids,
whereby students show language skills they have acquired through
knowledge and understanding. In the second section, students recite,
without a script, a piece of prose or poetry of their choice. The third
part involves reading out loud an extract from a book of the student's
choice, while the last part is a listening and responding section which
encourages the audience to react to whatever is said.'

As I recall, I took the English Speaking Board exam, somewhat reluctantly, in 1967, after my family moved from the Kirkcaldy Dialect area of Fife to Corby, Northamptonshire.

Lochty Bridge

The *tairsgear* (or tushker) is an implement used in Scotland for cutting peat.

★

Acknowledgements are due to the following publications: *Agenda*, *Literary Review*, *London Review of Books*, *Manhattan Review*, *New Statesman*, *Oxford Poetry* and *Poetry* (USA).

Some of the work here appeared in the pamphlet *Five Poems: An Essay on Mourning*, Clutag Press, 2018.

'Indelible' was commissioned for the Edinburgh International Book Festival *Throwing Voices* project and was performed, with music by Luke Sutherland, at the festival in August 2019.

'Cairn' and 'Hether Blether' featured in *Wild Music*, a radio collaboration with composer Erland Cooper, produced by Victoria Ferran of Just Radio and first broadcast on BBC Radio 4 in December 2019.

Special thanks to Agustina Bazterrica, Erland Cooper, Victoria Ferran, Alex Kozobolis, Michael Krueger, Piero Salabe and Luke Sutherland.